Also By Joeffrey Bartman

The Cave of Night (Solo Press) 1975

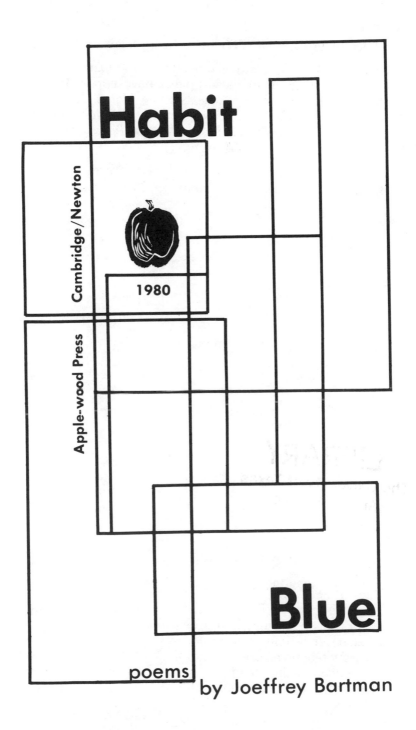

Habit

Cambridge/Newton

1980

Apple-wood Press

Blue

poems by Joeffrey Bartman

ACKNOWLEDGMENTS

Grateful acknowledgment is made to the following publications in which a number of these poems have appeared: *Arion's Dolphin, Butt, Bartlett Broadsides, Dark Horse, The Emerson Review, Grilled Flowers, Lynx, Nimrod, The North American Review, Penny Dreadful, Ploughshares, Poetry Northwest, Quarry, Snowy Egret, Spectrum.*

The poem "Power" was first published in broadside by the Broadside Bookshop in Northampton, Massachusetts.

Habit Blue © 1980 Joeffrey Bartman

ISBN: 0-918222-13-3 paperback

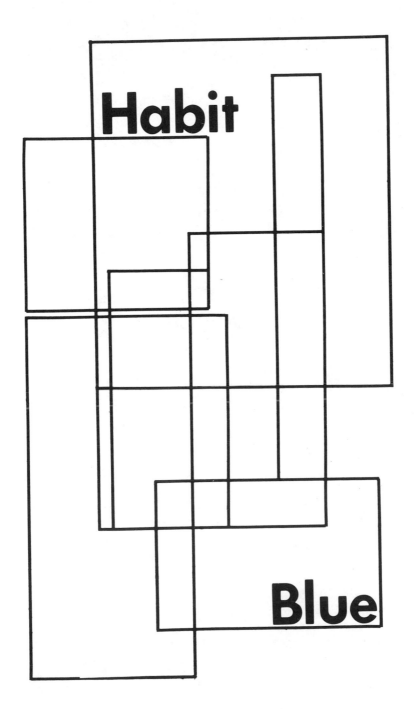

to my father

CONTENTS

A Science of Sympathy

11 Joker
12 The Trees Do This And That
13 Row Of Circles, Circle Of Hands
14 Next
15 I Am Blind, My Dog Is Dead
16 Picturing Marcilla
17 For Drinks On The Patio
18 Hardboiled In Daytime
19 Me
20 Poem
21 Snowdrifts
22 Foolery
23 Small Press
24 Wish
25 The Habit Of Chance

Flag

29 Mexico
30 From *The Lipstick Factory*
31 Speechless
32 Losing A Night Near Morning
33 City Nature
34 Oceanography
35 In '72 Shoichi Surrenders
     Prays For Japan And Goes Home
36 Mass General
37 The Baseball Player's Honeymoon
38 Of Something Near Cub Run
41 Instructions For Sunday Dinner
43 On The Fence

True North

47 Prix
48 Caesura Mobile
49 Recognizing
50 Power
51 Given

52 The Possible Call
53 This Is Not Us
54 Glasses
55 Apprentice Angel
56 The Gossiping Anonymous
58 The Little Death
59 In Place Of The Heart
61 Locus Novelle
62 What Could Be Silence

A Science of Sympathy

Joker

He's been everywhere with everyone
having a good cry. He's crossed the tracks
at quite a few points of no return.
He's never coming back again,
often. During a drought he went
knifing at a thundercloud and came away singing.
Over dinner he talks about his discoveries:
numerous isms, an alarm clock orange lovesick
pea pod guitar that smokes, something written
automatically. I didn't get it all.
He stays late looking to drug the hostess.

So assuming that with a fish hook
he can pull you out of your skin,
assuming he is happy with the feel of your soul
curling in his fingers, and assuming that you,
out of control, burst your muscles
like bullets into glass, can we then assume
he has a reason for all this, understands it.

The orphaned heart wants an explanation.
Laughter answering the axe.
He writes only about himself
and even then he lies.

The Trees Do This
And That

The trees in the yard, the trees on the corner.
Peaches on a tree, blurred
in the rain, through a window.

The trees do sway, lean
in the wind, in the white and yellow sun.
They taunt themselves, each other
as sunset unbuckles their spines.

Undressing in the fog or waiting to be
undressed by the shadow of a houselight,
they try to burst the shotglass buried
deep in their centers. Wind trailing
a scarf between their sorry limbs.
People worn to hangings, ribbons to fairs.
Two bluejays rival near the trash.

The moon blinks, the trees woo,
the swaggering stars are ignored.
Rain meanders, blackens the bark. The trees
have spent lifetimes determining
summer for winter, spring for fall
and barricading night for day.

The oldest tree in the town and the tree
in the park tatooed by lovers. The trees
just planted. The trees on the orphanage lawn.
The trees in the forest. The one tree
we don't know about. The tree that does
or doesn't fall. The branches
tangled in the telephone wires
that parallel the highway.

Row Of Circles,
Circle Of Hands

I agree, a light inside us
is pulsing its white water.

And there is an apple
wheeling itself throughout

and trying to do everything.
I know about a pine tree, chrome

glass, nervous with fireflies.
There is nothing like it.

It can listen, worse,
we can be ignored. Talk

about the snail in the brain
trying to be a crow.

The melancholy carriers of earth, dull,
memorializing the same old same old.

I've lost track of my paperweight eyes
looking forever in the right place.

The intelligent animals wintering it out
glowing around the fire lanterns of survival.

Their own breath wraps them like skins.
Once, in a snowstorm, I walked a bridge

over a highway and a river from my hometown
to inward, to endless.

I agree about the light
and the magic of the fish inside

alive with the pleasure
of dividing again.

Next

Let's talk about failure.
It followed me home expecting dinner.
I warmed up some left over dilemma
and we discussed my future.
Oceanic noplace.
Telephoto blank blank.
Low watt streetlamp.
Abundant miasma.
Sick and tired of:
Learning something from this.
Failure smoked a cigar
and continued to improvise.
It was like a rainy Sunday with everybody
reading a different section of the news.
Afternoon ended it all in grey.
The evening was a failure,
no beer, no snacks, burnt chili.
Boredom had a streetfight with the TV.
Perhaps sculpture? Simple: To sculpt a man,
chisel from a block of stone everything
that doesn't look like a man. Failure
said that now I was cooking with gas,
said give that a try, something, anything.

I Am Blind,
My Dog Is Dead

There is no one
to know what I'm up to.
I awake in the company of shadows
laddering across my face. The dark
is a riddle of harbingers and consequences.
The sky imagines a version of blue.
This is the world of my house,
the morning, day, the wind bending the
rhododendron toward the garage.

Tonight, four drinks drunk,
I am older by one year, traveling
in equal parts chase and escape.
An acceptable goodbye is impossible,
endings never satisfy.
Despondent is the gift of lonely.
Solitude on guitar.
I am blind, my dog is dead.
If you see me let me know.

Picturing Marcilla

She is the girl always pictured as running,
exhausting wheatfield after wheatfield
flapjack of sun after sun.

The skyline of corn the color of her hair.
How will she know me: slowly and more slowly.
Her address: evening.

Precise Dakota snow geese fly an arc
over a grain elevator seven miles east of US 40.
Her eyes as empty as nobody's mirror.

For Drinks On The Patio

The yellow of the buglight
from the porch glares
on the chinaberry tree.
The house inside seen through
every well-lit window alive
as the face of a stopwatch.
Ray pumps Debbie for info about Jane.
Now: a door will slam meaningful
but misunderstood. It loses
a few volts in the retelling.
Car keys on a ring
in the pocket of somebody's pants.
Let's get a dose of rain in down here,
down in the blackout of
my disassembled backyard.

Hardboiled In Daytime

Night came to hang around
me solo and bluesy
about the tomorrow business.
Sunset smeared her make-up
in the parking lot. Profundity,
I thought, days bite the dust.
I wondered on a stone's many
fingers and on a local water
beetle passing like a small
black shoe. Drugstores. Half
a dozen unemployed watchdogs
approach the mouth of the newsstand,
spit some nonsense on the black
tile headlines. How to explain
the geography of my lassitude
what with darkness.

Me

A clothesline of pajamas fattened
by the breeze laughs in the sun. That's
me on the curb with my gold finger
and my mesmerist's eye. Art,
I say, is a bracelet lost
at the supermarket. Yes it's me
who says: For you, because
the hills are not green or blue-green
or purplish blue, I have you a
new color here. It's called "hills"
and its color you see with eyes shut.
Where else could it be?
The eyes are so crucial,
the hills are such hills.

Poem

It is blue and
surrounded by itself.
It is green, square
now somewhere else
and red. It is not
a mark joining other marks
on a raft of air someplace.
It makes sense when touched.
It is triangular. It is
everything including simple.
It is not a circle
yet now then.

Snowdrifts

Drive across the overpass and then
along the flats where the women
asphyxiating in their underground sleep
awaken to crazily throw off the sheets.

Foolery

Friends visit and damn
if we don't catch ourselves again
tactless on embarrassment's keyboard.
The hydrolics of grace
succumb to emotional scurvy.
We redo our accidents, we toy
with our criminal stupidity.

We stick in our thumbs and pull out a
temper tantrum, wrestle the screen door
to a single hinge. Out come our obsessions,
their fat middles like tidbits in a candy dish.

"Getting things done occurs only on a schedule."
"Nothing worth learning can be taught except by example."

Poems to the taciturn you, the imperceptible me.
On the tip of somebody's tongue
jibberish odes salute our privacy.

Hell, we suspend our charms and heads
get smithereened like kegs of wine.
I look for in you a questionably ecstatic
moth inside a lampshade. On a ridiculous cruise
in a ridiculous dream, we feel ridiculous
and move toward the obvious conclusion.

Small Press

There are shadows and blue
where my letterpress tiles
stack into a maze. Cornering
light glares on the plates
and I get set to print
the whole shebang of history.
Children flower in my ear
etching their sharp youth
on a highway out of town.

O scribbler demographics!
Escapist, bibliographer,
somnambulist, outdoorsman.
I give you a typeface named Babytooth,
a bold italic named Lazybones. See them
on horseback Palamino Serif.

Tintoretto Roadsign announces that
the asphalt will curve. Advertising
packages sample Compacta Light.
Ubiquitous Helvetica Medium.
I grew up on Futura Display,
went to a Microgramma School,
failed Pluto Outline and love, Grotesque
remembers Desdemona Solid, Duelette
Juliet Capulet Romeo Montague.

Over-inked rollers on the first magazine.
Typos in the psychopath's best paragraph.
I put this all together singing: Goosedown,
Microfilm, Multiquadrata. Singing
Anapest, Doubleknit, Strophe, Strophe.

Wish

I sleep in only flares so far
I sleep the sleep for the moment
of the dragonfly passing me once
in a blue moon. My wish sleeping easier
than the canoe paddling the river,
the pen licks the inkwell.
My nights are braced
with the energy of hours up,
the age of a long time. Uncertain
I say sleep in the classroom
of lovers won't do. I want
the sleep of tiring work
the dream, easy to remember
difficult to have.

The Habit Of Chance

On loan to the unexplainable
I make do with painkillers.
The afternoon states its policy
about rented rooms: By the day
and programmed with grey forevers.

All four seasons appear
in the way a rainstorm gathers.
They are confused in an hour.
Poems writing themselves sick
present a grid of nerves
in a glass of water.

This house is hidden with angel bats
frozen to the rafters and raingutters.
They leave nosebleeds in the snow and soon
their skulls and the rags of their wings
will be carried on a blow of wind.

Necessity writes one on a scrap of paper
about apples baking in a brickoven about
setting fire to a nest of hornets
larger than a cider jug and spun
into the green thick of the hedge.

Most thoughts come blue passing
like miles of half-light shadows,
unimportant though luminous
through the thin glass
in the lamp of the head.

On the blue ice of my personality
monotony will spend itself. I wait
quietly and then blame the quiet,
waiting for it all to be interesting
again, and beautiful and new.

Flag

Mexico

One woman
falling asleep
racing a dream
of priceless stones,
of jackpots.
In her clothes
she appears gnarled,
muscular, still as a bead
in a pill vial.
Mexico. The harmless maraca.
The raving piano.

From *The Lipstick Factory*

In the door and taken for the
shift getting off. We slap a fog
of dust from our corduroys,

wipe our hands in our hair.
Another set of eyes trades a photo
with another set of eyes. A local

mouth howls when it gets bingo.
A few puckering others kiss sloppily. The girl
is in love with the guy. The girl

is not in love with the guy. Two guys
are in love with the same girl. Another girl
loves somebody else or at least says she does.

A guy loses. A girl wins. Vice versa.
All combinations cross wired.
Two girls bicker over the daredevil who said hello.

A girl and a guy whisper that the money's
got to go for snowtires. One waitress in two
uniforms takes up three seats. Haloes

of our pink dust dream on the ceiling.
Eyelids and underneath puffed up
like a blouse full of wind. I breathe

long and short in emergency red. Blowouts
air guns and wristwatch alarms.
The jukebox, it revs. Eggs

fry and squeal and hams boil and cry.
A rack of saucepans falls on the griddle
and clangs slowly like a trainwreck telling itself

to a town via snow. Cuddling in houses
embracing mountains, the sleepers
they almost hear.

Speechless

Calm fractures and splits
with every heartbreak overheard.

Windows glaze up and the moon
slivers to an edge of ice. I can't

talk worth a damn. No color. Dull
to memory and its distance of rope.

Helpless as speechless can be.
Twosomes pass with no letup. Look

at those two, last night they were halves
of another two. I drink teardrops

behind the wheel in car after car.
My wristwatch shines its sassy dial in the dark

picking up on a bladeful of headlight.
My shirtsnaps crack open and shut too.

I should write a book and make it into a movie.
I should fuck the book and start the movie.

Dressed in the truest camouflage blue
I'll stand tongue-tied on a platform of blanks.

A burglar caught mouthing the hundred
angles of her jewels.

Losing A Night
Near Morning

Barely within earshot
a single whimper wraps
your spine in a shiver:
a phone line from you
to a distant hyena.
Our own box of luck
disassembled far away.

The queen moon cringes
a last reflection derailed
awry on the linoleum.
Vapor overlaps vapor
until clouds staggering
drop the fog.

City Nature

The light changes flickering
like money falling on the sidewalk.
In each window's black hand lamps
go on flaring like yellow cards.
The streets are not surprised by night.
The park benches accept their blue
sweaters. A blackbird's wing
the last shadow. A cat
at the back door waits for
licks at a milkbowl. No sign of sleep
in the armchair near the fireplace.

Oceanography

It is a sea meter
set way down, nestled
in some half-live shells.

An oval of amber light
with a serene white
needle inside
like a keepsake
strand of hair
sheltered in a locket.

The casual move from zero
as a school of
pewter-colored fish
pass in their own wedge
of the sea.

In '72 Shoichi Surrenders Prays For Japan And Goes Home

Another starving day
eats itself. Tonight in a
picture frame you will be
one more cross-legged

man beneath a lightbulb
reading the book of your hands.
In your hut
in a bamboo thicket

your friends argue until they
move away, argue until they starve.
You find this crazy and hang
their skins out to dry.

There stand the departed spirits,
saying: "Why are you
returning home alone
leaving us here marooned?"

You eat twenty-eight years worth
of nuts, mangoes, papayas, red rats,
frogs, salmonberries, treebark, scallions.
Dream of miracles, secrets

and of women.
Don't build fires that spell out
words on the beach. You and an
airplane don't get along either.

But when a coconut offers you
a pair of its own stringy pants,
you take them. It will be years
before you can get them on.

Meanwhile, you steal a
cute and tiny jacket from a
raindrop pixie. Bits of spoon as
buttons catch the sun exactly.

Mass General

Down with fever
but frosted as a beermug.

Some who-knows variation
caught by splashing around

in the grim sludgy dust bowl
of every breath and everybody.

Caught by the blink of an eye.
A cloud called music

threatens with its fiddle,
burning a radium bald spot

onto the top of my head. My lungs
get aired like pillowcases.

I haul my pigeon-egg eyes
over to a glass of orange juice.

Cure myself by rivet gunning pill
after pill, no way. You cure me

with your eyedroppersworth of breezes.
Cure me with the ordered tablets

involved, white handfuls
like spares of your own teeth.

Me downwind of you
as the bed gets remade.

Will I ever kick this
terminal forever.

Days. Weeks.
I'm a dreamboater.

The Baseball Player's Honeymoon

He remembered the one in a million mouth-pink melon ball dropping off his toothpick onto the lawn. It was some wedding his wedding, him all smiles and being ribbed left and right. He got himself a wife himself. He kills his last highball with one long pull.

She drops her skirt and steps out of it as if avoiding a puddle. She heads for the john, her fanny sagging in her synthetic panties like the last two grapefruits in a plastic bag. He notices her chubbiness vanish as she reaches to brush the length of her hair. She has prickly little armpits and she has ribs. The staircase of her spine. And as she turns on the faucet her nipples sit like two red hats thrown on a sofa. Her suitcase is open on a chair, exposed are the components of a white and bewildering mechanism of underwear.

Boxes hideously wrapped and colored, piled like unfilled bleachers. More hotels is what he mumbles from the bed. He sits there real still awhile tracing the slow lob of each drop of condensation as it slides off the ice bucket. To the left of the bed it's his own shadow that he dreams into.

The good news of a hard-earned bonus for so many RBIs. His over-equipped Barracuda takes hometown corners. Jersey relentlessly churning its notion of suburbia. A champ and his family do TV, endorsing everything breakfasts and anything instant, in a kitchen glazed with formica and fluorescent with linoleum. The utility infielder has an icemaking Kelvinator and kids whose blood is laced with enough OJ to get sunstroke. Flabbergasted that she has peach fuzz to be bleached, swamps her spit scurls in a jism of styling gel. She's throwing curves out there umpire.

And she appears from the bathroom in frightening feather slippers and a white peignoir. It's her reflection that turns in the glass of the sliding door like a sailboat capsizing in a tear.

Of Something Near
Cub Run

You swat a bug off a ham shank
Meats hang in the attic like
a row of stairs to another floor.
You are up here to get a chair
so you can sit outside if you want.

The little butterfly pins your
daughter makes are in rows in a box.
Three were sold already this weekend.

There will be a party maybe in a day.
This is what the dogs know as they
group outside the kitchen door. After
a meal of scrapple they snooze.

For two seasons you've refused to buy
a cord of wood. The brothers fill their
pockets and even their gloves with tinder.
They plan to take the cousins to the snake
and monkey farm nearby in Sweeny.

Crocheted doilies are on the table.
They go under the bone china
cracked, chipped and stained
like a row of old man teeth.

You try to close the flue in the chimney, can't
so you build a fire, the fuel is furniture.
The wood burns jade smokey blue
green and I see the ocean.
Lupe, who shaves the pigs and slits their throats,
helps you rip the stumpy legs off an armchair.
A cripple stands flapping in the family room
limber, dancing as if imitating an animal.

The kitchen door opens: a farm walks in,
then some trucks, small stores, some beer fed
sheep, overalls, dungarees, checked shirts, hats.
Folks tap corn and callous plagued feet to a banjo
and fiddles. Short women, their hairdos blossoming
at the shoulders of their men. Oh the romance
when she hugs his arm. White frills dip and
swivel circling partners. A straight pin
holds her collar down.

The siblings are tired of daddy's shoestore.
The cowboy stockboy outside throws his lasso
at a fencepost during the sing along.
He's a loner and hustles dillies on the sly.
He complains: "I hate the store too. I can't
never get them alligators out of the boxes and once
a damn lapis lazuli came on back to life!" He's troubled
and been up nights sucking the blue turtles of insomnia.

Everybody doesn't like what they eat.
Brother's flannels itch and his potatoes
are too hot. You start taking pills
causing headache notions
of developers bulldozing the smokehouse
and laconic roadsigns that storytell.

Instead of arguing let's all just tell stories.
   "In 1912 Fu Toy Ling came from the old country. He spoke no
English but managed to open a grocery store in Washington
State. Indians came in, they were housed at a nearby reserva-
tion, farmed hops and sweet cherries, drank whiskey and ate
government steak. Fu had a long ponytail in the Cantonese
style. The Indians had two ponytails, couldn't tell what tribe he
was from and never trusted him."

the only daughter
talks love but cuts
the deck at crazy.
The fire that is her hair.
In the city,
subways through a grate
in the sidewalk, maybe a
vacuum through an open window.
See the umbrellas up in the air and
a steam leak through a crag in an alley.
I want
to walk her around in tall buildings.
Settle down with a phobia in a highrise,
get a job and taxi to it and from it
passing her asleep in a shaded doorway
celebrating fatigue after her somersault.

Instructions For Sunday Dinner

Take two stones and one egg. Disregard them until one can't be told from the other. When this has happened, find a deer, a buck. Kill him somehow but leave him there. Hide in the bushes for a while. A hunter will soon come along complete with caution-yellow cap and insulated snake boots. He'll take the deer for his own, guaranteed. You know hunters. Watch your deer as he rides home tied to a fender.

Raymond Chandler believed certain foods to be beneficial to the process of writing and others to be a hindrance. The foods he claimed would put lead in your pencil are: fresh trout, black olives, young lamb roasted with thyme, beef stew only when a cup of dark beer is added as it simmers, wild mushrooms, bear, venison, and rabbit. Things to stay away from, foods that'll keep you all backed up like tunnel traffic are: cultivated greens, canned soups, overcooked pasta, dry roasted nuts and anything frozen. So eat accordingly. Nonsense, Chandler's full of shit. Writers are just like other people except that they believe in things less strongly.

Here are some excellent recipes for duck:

Duck a la Creme: Begin by carefully removing the bones, feathers, skin, fins, scales, hair, hubcaps, etc. Inflate the bird with a handy bicycle pump. Prepare a standard white sauce of paint and corn flour. Submerge the duck in it and cook for six days over a blast furnace. Wrap in flypaper and serve.

Duck Albanian: Take a plump duck to the barber and have him given a shave and haircut or if it's a female, given a facial, manicure and permanent wave. Before killing, stuff with three butt ends of salami and an oily rag. Prepare a gravy of rubbing alcohol and dust. After strangling it with a horseshoe, lay the bird out on the table and call up some Albanian in the neighborhood to tell you what to do next.

Leftover Duck: This is one of the simplest and most useful of the bunch. Although not chic it tells us how to get the most for our money. Take the leftovers, or if there are none take the dirty plates, the greasy knives, forks and spoons, the soiled napkins, the belches, burps, sneezes, coughs and farts and stew them in milk of magnesia till the cows come home. Add moth balls and make sandwiches.

On Sunday get to the dining room early. Take a seat in the corner next to the buffet, you know in front of the cornice with the milkglass dishes. As Daddy divvies yams and Granma unwraps all the baked goods that have been waiting, light a stick match on your fingernail, light the tablecloth. Wait an hour or two and then, somewhere else, remembering, love the pecan pie and the decanter full of whatever it was.

On The Fence

There you are, directing each love-packed iceflow toward a truckstop somewhere down the white road of the heart. The different roads marked kinds of weather. You and your madcap laugh and the yelling: Take me out of Henrico County! Lips! Lips! Swallow me whole! It's a knee slapper, it knocks you over. And your big fanny hits the dirt like an innertube, a scare to the chickens. Shoo! Vamoose! And you whoop and flail those tickly fingers and the chickens they cluck and whoop too and fan their sides with their glovelike wings. So, you get up, sweep off your dusty jeans and tighten your belt a notch. Don't we know the dilemma. Gosh, what in hell is a television set. Do those chickens have lips. What's the antidote for immunity? Forever putting up with this avalanche of touches, every white hand coming down like a wand and not one carries a blessing, money or a new way of life. Who're all these pretty ladies, I can't do a thing.

True North

Prix

Crows in clouded light circle
neglected corn in a field

as slow winter develops its motion
the wind notes the season and the brushy
look of the trees and the grasses grow
defer to the yellow side of brown.

I hear that the planets and the sun

I hear that a bear can go for a week
dragging a wound inside trying to digest it
swallow the ravine hacked in its stomach.
A way explaining what today has been
and the night before.

Could be word in conversation.
Could be thought decoding reading.
Could be dream of past and future,
a sequence of bulbs on a length of wire.
If I am end to this woman
we keep it to each other.

We share our crowded hearts
but your nightmare is
your nightmare. And mine
goes back to me. The heat of my
breathing, my history of dark
where all the women cry
the man is mine.

Caesura Mobile

In the beginning I cut out paper dolls
and so did the man before me.

My uncle hid paper dolls in his shirt during the war
to help him remember his family.

Freud cut out paper dolls, left them
overnight on his desk claiming they did his work.

My father sent letters to his paper doll
written on paper dolls.

Once I asked a woman to . . .
She must have been a paper doll.

Paper dolls linking arms float
like ribbons over my bed, like dancers

at a wedding where they do not belong.
Their legs move in their skirts as if in a bell.

A few are ugly and fall asleep in my groin.
Others brush disgust through my hair.

I have never cut out the same paper doll twice.
They are as different as everyone's mother.

Paper dolls to dance with, to sing with,
paper dolls to read to me.

Some are intricate and beautiful,
some are simple and beautiful.

Many have left me, others I've given away
regretting both kinds of loss

with a paper doll called loneliness.
Those of heartbreak suffer many things

amnesia is not one. A silhouette
comes by surprise and I love it.

The paper doll scissored alone,
her face like a page of braille.

Recognizing

It is morning in the brain.
Mosquitoes buzz in your blood.
Shadows moving down a page of the newspaper
and a rose bush pops a nail from its trellis.

You look for another way to remember
as if groping for a lightswitch
among a variety of recognizable memories.
Knowing yourself in masks, you know yourself
in mirrors as they turn their backs.

Power

Storm slaps the roof.
The axe of night splits one room
into another. Her eyes blank as eggcups
give up on information. I can't
hide this, my ice on her cheeks of coal.
She's had enough of not enough.

The rain quitting removes its last bracelet.
I'm a letdown and anger too
has let her down. She whispers
nothing and is done with me
like a kid finished with some
broken cradle toy.

We are two rooms
each with their closets.
I look to live in the whole
space of a house, prepared
for a tenancy till doomsday.
I talk about tools needed
not why build at all.
I am this kind
with my wastebasket heart.
And this I think is power
but you, you take it back.

Given

I've shot the dog that's
been at the chickens all summer.
His dead eyes barely shining in the dark.
Me in the yard, in my underwear,
under half a moon. I drag him
to the foot of the back stairs.
You watch through the screen door.

But this won't mean a thing.
And no ocean of beer kept cold till drunk.
Not the winnings from some turkey shoot or a
mouthful of ten penny nails driven in three.
We've tried the sofa and on the floor
and yeh the kitchen sink but even there
it's no good. The oak floorboards
creaking beneath the bed
are what she listens for
all night. What she wants bucks
up stiff as a utility pole.
It runs like a vein of ice
toward her spine and it bites
back with her own teeth.

The Possible Call

Our voices time each other
the slow exchange, the quick one
the response that hesitates
doing tiptoe on the wire.
The trouble with this phone is:
you call, you don't call
or you get called. On my side
not admitting to the billion
tangles. If I didn't answer
after two rings the phone the phone

after four who in hell could it be
after five Susan with another alternative or
Linda beautiful and alone with her refrigerator
after seven rings it's Françoise taking me
to Nice for the next ten years
eight rings my dead Uncle's millions
for the rest of my life. Who'd
let it ring so damn many times?
Ten rings. It's God saying
hey motherfucker, hey dude...

I can remember what
your fist would grab
the knuckles of your small fist
white like an apple core
as you grab the saddle horn
or the small animal.

This Is Not Us

This is not us, really.
This is not us unreally. Watching
each other in the sun
more color than light.
The slate of our eyes.

This is not us
each opinion posted
anti, a splitting weakness.
The warped spruce beam
in the floor of this house.

What are our mistakes.
Is the end here or is it
here. Monitor the end.

Finished by the desire
to be over. This is
not us. We are not
contortionists strangling
in our own arms. This
is not us, really.

Glasses

Here full moonlight snows
its net of stars. Time revolves
like a bowl of ripening pears.
I bury my head into night's
dumb black sofa.

Glasses frighten easily on tables.
Colored napkins and silverware
set them glistening. Children's eyes
make them ring. Cars outside
and the windows hum.

Glasses relax elegantly wet,
half filled, gold and eventually tired.
Geese accumulate near a slow river.
A few slip into the air and gear their arc
over a shy white sailboat embarrassed
by the wind. The guy in the boat smokes,
sees a woman, discovers a future.

You and I forget whose glass is whose.
We mouth each other's lip mark on the rim.
The risk is only if we kiss our own.

Windshields, windows, they're glass.
Ice confuses me. Her eyes are more
than glass but her hair is glass
for sure. Her porcelain skin. Birds too,
especially blue ones and they have
a blue glass sky. The 400 some odd
miles of turnpike between us are glass.
Distance is glass, you know that.
Write a letter, make a call, light the eye
of a perfect red glass bell.

Apprentice Angel

We are done being so smart,
worrying about continuity.
Chaos can be charming.
The allure, unlimited.
No mind only temperament.

We faked it, whatever love was.
Whatever kept us warm
we called it drink. We sang and slept,
took a lucky number on a dream.

The streets were the grey of the world
of the sky. The instrument wind
of metal on metal. We used trouble
as another name for opportunity. Like
father like son by any other name.
A namesake fuming dust.

You know, you can make a name for yourself.
Get some loose brunette
aware that you're a sleeze, a liar
in a cockfight with truth.
Have a kid for every year of your life.
Name the boys Counterfeit and the girls Cold.

Untrue. No chance when your money
won't make honey, when you're flat out numb
and trying to act sober. Fool.

Promise we'll always know who we are
and we'll never starve. Promise
you'll love me with your nothing
and I'll live with that.
Promise me, apprentice angel,
that we'll get together
just for laughs.

The Gossiping Anonymous

I'll manipulate my own legend thank you.
Recently one of a red he-witch the magic
all run down. Long time confidant
of rainbows but the secrets start to pale.
Angrier than the snake who married
the garden hose. Next year undergone
employing minimal anaesthetic.

Lights sink into faces.
The generated gossip is illuminated.
History goes into shock.
Sparrows hunt worms.
The sparrows are chocolate sparrows.
The worms claim they are chocolate worms.
That's admiration. This is poetry
and the miserablisms are excruciating.
Poverty, shame, lost love, poor health,
anonymity, dandelion soup and shoe leather stew.
I'm a rumor in my own time.

I reach for a wishbone's hand
like a housewife for a dish rag,
I know nothing will occur. Not a threadbare
allowance of luxury, not a crack
at temptation. A drowsy ray of sunlight
travels the floor. I haven't seen a movie
in months but who cares when your whole
life's flashing before your eyes anyway.

In the streets of belladona the dummies move
to vacate their horizontal places.
A stethescope bothers with another
dull heartbeat, little commotion is made.
The truth uncovers its treasure of significance
and grieves quizzically in the form of laughter.
The wheels and pins in the stomach of a clock.
Swans, three of them in a pool in a park
are in love with each of their shimmering halves.

Tomorrow the weather will be boring
and bent on playing dead. Another
attempted half-assed suicide attempt
bleeps a would-be ending
across the red grass of somebody's brain.
But the story takes its own direction,
sets nothing straight
trying to clarify celebrity.

The Little Death

Sleep exaggerates on its sad calliope. No kidding. I know dreams are out of fashion but this is the dream where everybody you've ever known gets together. In the first paragraph we have Reality playing a big part and exhausting all involved. I don't remember what I say. What do I do? I leave at the end. I am unhappy. I am afraid and uncomfortable socially. I am told that I am able to manage. I manage. The spiders in my ego weave me a rope ladder escape out of Victimville. I talk to myself and I sound worried. I am sick, depressed, running with my eyes closed, searching, waiting, lacking imagination, confused and without a solution. I am told that I will come out of it, as always. I forget what is said, as always. Perhaps nothing is said but something slips in just under the wire. The coil of misunderstanding unwraps between the eyes. Sadness. Everything comes just in time, at the same time, sleep, the little death, the dead, just in time for death.

In Place Of The Heart

I've drowned love like a pillowcase full of kittens.
My family crossed the bridge and was gone.
A letter penned in whiskey
details from a cowboy's backyard.

Tell me one more time what my pseudonym is,
my *nom de plume*, how do you spell it.
Tell me you're in love with a lunatic
seeking employment as a lunatic.
Do I have any last words? Of course:
skin, hair, collarbone, nape of the neck,
ocean, her ocean.

Bippy, what did we expect?
Brandy in the bathtub and novocaine kisses.
You've been foggy lately with jewelry
and dream houses on your mind.
Balls of crystal. Me too,
but my future's been misplaced
like somebody's wallet.

Cookie Bunny, Bean, which half of the car do you want.
No, you take it. I can drive a sewing machine, sure.
Oh I didn't like food much anyway.
Don't wait up, I'll be back when I'm fifty.

You say that you are looking for Truth,
and when found, it will be almost circular.
Well, maybe you should take a sweater.
Without you the calm will be tumultuous.

She went to charm school, ballet school, a rich kid's
school, secretarial school, graduate school.
She was born on a horse and makes friends easily.
Everybody likes her. She never misses the point.
And you know what she told me:
This is the best world in the world.

Lyrics by the Beaner: Only you only you only you
only you...
Sonata for tuba and balloon
nickname for gloom
moon of wood
Duet for bookworm and lunatic
Backgammon and jazz
cookies
Backgammon and jazz

Locus Novelle

So much for heroes, even winter lies chained to its bed.
The house at night quiet as a gyroscope.
You can do what you want with the symbolism of water,
the You in the poem, the one rose, the unplanned.
The ample and the rickety are stymied by the same confusion.

Sometimes, I wish we could all just agree and go on home,
just get rid of it all, leave it alone.
However, I respect particular idiocy
during times of global idiocy.
The blind lead the blind
but everyone needs something to do.

Here, we are north of the trivial
east of our own good, our spirit
west of some otherness better forgotten
and we are south of
what we thought of.

What Could Be Silence

The long curtains blow into the room and light,
asleep in its moon house, has disappeared
and left me with what could be silence.
I forget everyone, everyone else.
Friends, blood relatives, current heartbreaks.
I forget money, I forget clothing in a pile
at the foot of the bed. I turn back the clock,
the blueprint for the melting of ice.
A diagram in memory's glass frosts over.
I forget my parents and they forget each other.
I fall in love but forget that.
turning in sleep, dreams forget themselves,
dreams are not forgotten.
The future rocks lurching
downhill like an overdue train.
Time takes its photograph and I am
different and I am the same. I forget
my life and my life remembers
and the long curtains blow into the room.

The Apple-wood Press began in January 1976. The image of the apple joined with the hard concreteness of wood in many ways expresses the goals of the press. One of the first woods used in printing, apple-wood remains a metaphor for giving ideas a form. Apple-wood Press books are published in the memory of Harry and Lillian Apple.